HOW TO WRITE A GREAT INFORMATION TECHNOLOGY STRATEGIC PLAN --
And Thrill Your CEO

Thomas S. Ireland

[Type text]

DEDICATION

To my son, Brendan,

who has been teaching me since he was very young.

Contents

ACKNOWLEDGEMENTS

With gratitude to those who have provided me with so many opportunities over the years.

Introduction

Who Is This Book For?

This book is written for the strategic planner who, if they do their job right, makes it possible for the rest of us to stay employed. The strategic planner's ability to envision clearly the future of the marketplace, the competition and the enterprise means the difference between long-term success and failure. The strategic planner's skill is vital, and their decisions may be of broader consequence than those of most others in the organization. Their ability to put all this information into a concise, clear, energizing, action-oriented Vision Statement can make the difference between organizational success or failure over the long term.

This book draws on my forty years of experience in information technology operations, program management and strategic planning. At the end of the book you will know how to establish, and energize people to follow, an Information Technology Vision that will support, and even enhance, the core mission and success or the enterprise you serve.

Why I Feel Compelled To Write This Book

I have written this book to pass along the result of a series of business and personal experiences and the teachings and guidance of some great mentors. All that I learned from those experiences and mentors provided a set of skills and knowledge about how to develop simple, clear information technology strategic plans supporting long term enterprise objectives.

1

Along the way, I've developed a set of rules I've listed on the next page that are useful for strategic planners and leaders.

Tom Ireland's Rules

- First Rule of Leadership: People will meet your expectations.
- Excellent leaders create excellent organizations.
- Delegate to the limit of your own guilt and other people's pain.
- Keep it simple because it will get complex all by itself.
- Murphy was an optimist.
- One aw shucks (or other word) wipes out a thousand attaboys.
- Technology is easy. Business change is tough.
- Technology without business application has no value.
- Never make a design decision for only one reason.

When I graduated from college, I had no idea that almost all of my career would involve long range, or strategic, information technology planning. As a commissioned officer and then as a civilian in the Air Force I spent most of 11 years as a telecommunications program manager working on multi-year upgrades and replacements of a wide variety of systems.

When I transitioned into industry, I went to work for what was, at that time, the world's largest on-line full-text search and retrieval system. The company was growing at 40% per year, and the data network was growing at 100% per annum. The data network had never fully met the demands of the business, and revenue was falling on the floor. The first year I was in this organization I felt like a total failure, and each day was a nightmare. I swore that I would never endure that nightmare again.

I studied that business inside and out. I was determined to understand the core enterprise I was serving! I worked with marketing, sales, finance, product managers and everyone I could to understand seasonal cycles and the annual growth predicted for various city markets across the country. I knew I had to develop a clear vision of where the business was going if I was going to survive, and if I was going to be a strong contributor to the enterprise's success. I used my engineering and project manager training to imagine, plan, cost out and successfully sell the idea of a network structure that would support the mission.

Revenue never fell on the floor again because of network under capacity. Nor was money needlessly spent due to creating too much capacity.

Soon after that I was tasked to join a small technology vision team at a major corporation. As a member of that team I knew we had to fully understand the present and projected mission and infrastructure of the core businesses. If we did that job well we would be able to present a Technology Vision and Infrastructure that effectively supported the core Enterprise Vision and Infrastructure. If we did our jobs with excellence we wouldn't just support the business, we would enhance it.

The effort was very successful. It was so successful that years after leaving that corporation and starting my own consulting business I was invited back with others on that Technology Vision team to celebrate the effectiveness and accuracy of that multi-year Vision and plan.

In my consulting business, we were often asked to take on a number of short-term projects, both simple and complex, and lead them for our customers. I was surprised to learn how few of our consulting customers had a coherent long-range IT plan integrated with a long-range core business plan. Most of the customers were aware of the planning need. However, they

3

either didn't think they had the time to spare or were unconscious of how much a good plan would help them. Many didn't have the skill for strategic planning and didn't know where to start.

This was quite a revelation. I had come from a series of organizations that were consciously aware of the need for strategic planning and that their plan needed frequent updating. Now I was encountering enterprises that were ignoring the need for one reason or another. Once some of these customers understood that my partner and I had the skill to do long-range planning we sometimes found ourselves with a new assignment to develop an information technology plan and integrate it with the business plan. Now I was doing planning work for organizations that had been relegating strategic planning to a low priority because they didn't have the time or the skill to dedicate to it.

This short book fulfills a great desire to share what I have learned. I will show you how the long-range planning tools presented here can help organizations improve customer satisfaction and their bottom line.

Planning Can Be Streamlined

Long-Range Planning Can Be Extremely Difficult

I'm going to show you how to make it easier!

Long-range planning, whether for two years or ten years, is difficult. If it was easy, every one of us wouldn't be making so many mistakes when predicting the future and charting long range courses for our businesses. Strategic planning is more challenging the further the plan extends into the future.

The everyday world presents us with a lot of variables. A mathematician might say that the task of long-range planning is a problem filled with many more variables than we have simultaneous equations, or information, needed to solve it. This implies that we can't arrive at a precise solution. A statistician might be quite comfortable with this situation and use the incomplete information to arrive with some specified degree of certainty at an answer within some bounds of probability. However, CEOs of companies are in the uncomfortable position of having to reject the answers of both the mathematician and the statistician.

The chief executive of an enterprise needs something more precise. The chief executive knows that the better their enterprise is at planning for the future the better their chance of being successful at beating the competition, increasing operating efficiency and effectiveness, and providing service that delights the customer. So, the person, or team, doing the long-range planning within the enterprise must be making better determinations about the future than the competition to assure success of their enterprise.

In this book, I will generally use the term "enterprise" to refer to the broad range of organizations that must do strategic

5

planning to succeed. This might be a small or large commercial business, a non-profit or a local, state or federal government agency. Sometimes I might call the enterprise a business or organization. Please assume that the terms are meant generically and are interchangeable. The process of long-range planning outlined in this book has been used successfully by the author in all of these types of organizations.

IT Teams Must Be Active, Not Reactive, Planning Partners

This book is about the role of the CIO and the CIO's staff in this process of long-range planning for the entire enterprise as well as for the IT organization within that enterprise.

For the CIO's staff, this can be a very tough challenge. The day to day operation of an information technology group is generally fast-paced and complex. Each person on the team is probably paying great attention to detail for their particular part of the technical systems to make sure everything keeps operating properly. The information technology staff is generally immersed in a day to day operation using technologies that change faster than is true in most other industries and for the core enterprise they are supporting.

The CIO's staff is multitasking intense day to day operations with periodic unexpected and critical events. At the same time, they are also routinely, or periodically, working to understand what is coming down the technology pipeline that might be applied to new requirements of the enterprise. There often isn't time, or sufficient breadth of skill within the team, to accomplish daily operations as well as long-term planning.

Those in the core business of the enterprise may be in a similar situation. They are also working to find a way to integrate long-range planning with daily operations. Everyone, no matter what their primary discipline, has to balance day to day operations with future planning. The number of team members available in this time of intense competition is often only sufficient to meet the needs of the daily operation with minimal resources left over for periodic future planning.

It is in the area of future planning that there can be a major difference between the CIO staff and the core business. Information technology is changing much faster than almost any other field. Unless rapidly developing technologies are a core part of the business, or are closely related to the enterprise's product, the changes coming at the core business team may not be as intense as they are for the CIO's team. This can create a cultural disconnect between the core enterprise planners and the IT planners.

However, it can also present an opportunity. The rapidly changing pace of information technology may provide an advanced, innovative tool to increase efficiency or accelerate the process of core product development. Looked at this way the IT staff may be able to increase significantly their value to the core business if they increase their understanding of, and integrate themselves ever more fully into, the end-to-end business processes.

The CIO and the CTO will almost certainly be properly focused on the business applications of technology. In their positions they will understand that technology is just a tool to support the enterprise.

However, chances are that even mid-level technology managers are striving so hard to keep up with technology evolution and operational reliability that they don't have much of an opportunity to channel their creative talents into looking

7

for new business applications of the technology they provide. In the crush of day-to-day activity they may find themselves in a reactive mode. It isn't unusual to find mid-level technology managers attending staff meetings in which they are told to quickly bring a new application on line that the CIO or CTO has determined is important to the mission of the business.

This can put the CIO, CTO and the entire IT team at a disadvantage. The CIO and the CTO are almost certainly losing their technical skills as they use more of their time to focus on the executive-level issues of the business they are supporting. As the mid-level IT managers work to keep up with their daily activities, a planning gap can open because the executive and mid-level groups may not have sufficient time to trade information to their mutual benefit. This can result in lost business opportunities and the need to create rush projects with shorter lead times than desirable to meet new goals.

In this book, we are offering a planning tool that effectively closes this gap. As the gap closes through use of this tool, the mid-level managers and the front-line workers will have a better view of the mission and Vision they are working to support. The CIO and CTO will have a working team that they can periodically, in a formal and efficiently structured way, draw into the business planning process. This gives the executive team a greater number of human resources to draw into the planning process and assures that the IT teams are strongly focused on technologies that support and enhance the enterprise mission.

Elements of the Planning Tool

Introduction to the Planning Tool

The tool offered in this book is one that consistently and firmly focuses each technologist's attention on support of the Enterprise Vision and mission. The premise of the tool is that "Technology without business application has no value".

We will talk throughout this entire book about Vision and Infrastructure. Please note that I've deliberately capitalized the first letter of each key word in this book, such as Vision and Infrastructure, to emphasize its importance in the planning process.

This tool assumes that every enterprise has a clearly documented Vision statement. At the very least there is an Enterprise Vision that can be estimated by the technology team even if it isn't written and documented by the enterprise.

It also assumes that every enterprise has a framework within which it operates that can be called the Infrastructure. In order for the IT team to support fully the Enterprise Vision and Infrastructure, they need to define an Information Technology Vision and Infrastructure for their own team that is focused primarily on the core Enterprise, not on developing technologies.

Vision and Infrastructure are presented in this book as the pillars of a straightforward, proven way to create an IT Strategic Plan that fully supports, and can enhance, the Business Strategic Plan. You will be presented the following sketch later in this book. I'm showing it to you now so you will know where I am leading you.

9

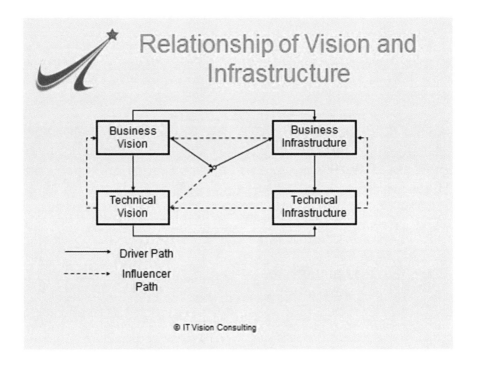

As you read this book, please pay close attention to the four terms presented in this sketch.

- <u>Business Vision</u> is the long-range objective that the top enterprise executives have established for the entire enterprise. This Business Vision sets the stage for Business Infrastructure, Technical Vision and Technical Infrastructure.
- <u>Business Infrastructure</u> is the organizational structure and environment of the entire enterprise. It results from the Business Vision and the leadership style of the chief executive.

- Technical Vision is developed by the chief IT executive in cooperation with the enterprise executive team. It is based on, supports, and may enhance the Business Vision.
- Technical Infrastructure is built by the IT team to support the Business Vision and Infrastructure, and the Technology Vision.

Using the process described in this book you, the planner, will follow this sequence of events.

First: examine and understand the Business Vision for the core enterprise you are supporting.

- Second: fully understand the Business Infrastructure that has been created at the direction of the executive team to support that Business Vision. (Everything always comes back to the Business Vision!)
- Third: as a technologist supporting the Business Vision you will develop and implement a Technical Vision and,
- Fourth: you will create a Technical Infrastructure that supports, and preferably enhances, the Business Vision.

It is important to reemphasize that the purpose of this book is to provide a proven framework for establishing an Information Technology Vision and an Information Technology Infrastructure that fully supports the Vision and Infrastructure of the core business.

I've applied the tool described in this book repeatedly over decades with total success. It works!

Keep it simple because it will get complex all by itself

A concern with long-range planning is that it can be very time-consuming and often be too challenging. This may be especially true for IT people who already deal with a complex technology which is threatening to become more complex at an accelerating rate. A rule I have developed and use with my teams is "Keep it simple because it will get complex all by itself".

The planning method described here is straightforward. It contains two primary elements: Vision and Infrastructure.

The executives who run the core enterprise determine the Business Vision and Business Infrastructure with some influence from the environment in which the business exists.

The IT people have a task with a somewhat different flavor. The supporting IT Vision and Infrastructure they have to come up with is, as we will see in this book, dictated by others. "Others" in this case means the business executives who are deciding the direction of the business, and the technology companies in the world who are developing and introducing products at exponentially accelerating rates.

There must be a strong effort to keep things simple at the beginning the planning effort. Otherwise, the task of the IT team could spin into unmanageable complexity. And this happens with some teams. Setting Enterprise Vision and Infrastructure as the base platform, and returning all investigation and extrapolation to that platform, is an excellent and proven way to keep complex things as simple as possible.

Technology without business application has no value.

It might be wise at this point to get some technology "heresy" out of the way. This book is written for technologists, but a major premise of this book is that technology is inherently valueless. We can create all the technology we want, but if it doesn't serve some useful business purpose it has no point.

All of us who are in technology were probably initially attracted because the tools (toys?) of technology are so cool. Almost all technologists get great fun out of designing new systems, operating complex networks and looking ahead to the next invention that they get a chance to work (play?) with. Hopefully, as we progress in our careers, our enjoyment of technology continues and increases but with a stronger focus on the application of technology to core enterprise needs. For the technologist supporting an enterprise (private, public, non-profit, etc.) it is this application of technology to business that brings real value.

Chief executives are always working on business change in response to market variations, fresh opportunities, product evolution and a number of other planned and unplanned factors. It is this business change that creates new and increasing value. Those who handle this change the best are ones who perform better in the eyes of the customer compared to the competition. We will spend a good amount of this book describing the role the technology team plays to facilitate and enhance this business change needed to create the new and increasing value.

Business leaders are increasingly aware that technology can enable business change. Those business leaders who understand this best are the ones who are demanding that their CIO and their IT team become entrenched in the business planning process and be change agents for the business.

Technology is easy. Business change is tough.

13

Another piece of heresy, from the perspective of many technologists, is that technology is easy - business change is tough.

Information technology teams install voice, wireless, network, data and computing systems and provide them as tools and systems to help people get their daily tasks done. That is challenging stuff to install properly and keep working on a daily basis. However, the technologist who is fully integrated into the business of the enterprise will soon realize that the real challenge is using the technology to bring marketplace value through business change.

The CIO and team who bring the full power of technology value to the business will dramatically improve the enterprise's position in their industry and the position of the IT team in their enterprise. That is the real thrust of this book!

Now that the heresy is out of the way it is important to make it clear that this book takes pains to describe things in a systems approach because the people this book is written for are systems oriented. This book describes a process that integrates the CIO team into the core business planning process. It meshes IT Vision with Business Vision and IT Infrastructure with Business Infrastructure. Along the way, Business Vision and Infrastructure are enhanced by the CIO's team to bring greater value to the business than would have been realized otherwise.

The "old AT&T" used to have a motto: "The System is the Solution". That is pretty much the point here. The CIO team's technology solutions merge with the business solutions into a single system for the enterprise.

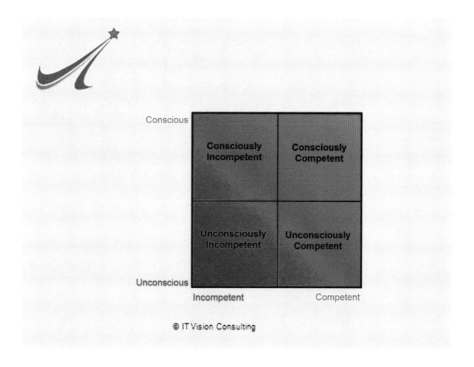

Individuals and organizations range from being unconsciously incompetent to consciously competent. Some of you have encountered the matrix shown above. For those who haven't it is worth a short discussion and analogy.

We have all encountered automobile drivers who are unconsciously incompetent. Those are the ones who frequently receive the "one fingered salute" and don't have a clue about what they did wrong as they create havoc when driving down the road. They sometimes cause car accidents around them that they aren't even aware of. These are the people who don't drive; they intermittently aim. At some point, they injure themselves or others and pay outrageous insurance rates. In business, these unconsciously incompetent are the people and companies that fail miserably and are quickly eliminated from the competitive arena.

The unconsciously competent are the drivers who have driven for quite a few years and are almost on autopilot. They have great skills but do things so automatically that they may periodically lose some awareness of what is going on around them. Perhaps many of us lapse into this category from time to time. Maybe you have had the experience of driving down the road for a few miles and not being able to remember what happened over that distance. These drivers may get into trouble in spite of their skill. In the business world the enterprises that fall into this category may succeed, but they will never be at the top of the heap.

Then there is the consciously incompetent driver who has no skill and knows it. They are either the brand-new driver or someone who just can't develop good driving skills. Those who can't develop driving skills are always bumping into things, and their car is full of dents and dings. They don't get the damage fixed because they are well aware that it is meaningless to do so. They get quite a few tickets and accept them gracefully. They may work to improve their skills so they can become consciously competent, but they may or may not succeed in that goal. The business in this category will fade if they don't fix their incompetence because their customers will eventually abandon them. However, because they are conscious of their shortcomings, they could be well positioned to move to being consciously competent assuming they ask for help from experts.

The consciously competent are at the top of the heap. These are the skilled drivers who know the laws, know their cars, are aware of their limitations and keenly observe what is going on around them, so they can drive defensively. They may be so aware that they can almost sense impending errors by others and put space between themselves and a potential accident. They are continuously improving their skills and listen to the constructive criticism of others. They may even be practicing improving their skills, attention and reaction time in competitive events. In business this is the company that is outstanding! However, they are only outstanding because they are aware that it is easy to slip into unconscious competence and lose their edge. Consequently, they are always in a continuous improvement process to avoid moving out of the top right quadrant. They know that it is dangerous to get comfortable with their position and their skills.

The planning tool being presented in this book is as much a tool for remaining consciously competent as it is a tool for excellent strategic planning.

The Vision And Infrastructure Matrix

The Vision and Infrastructure Planning Matrix

Here is another chart that you will see again toward the end of this book. I want to show it to you now so you will know where I am leading you.

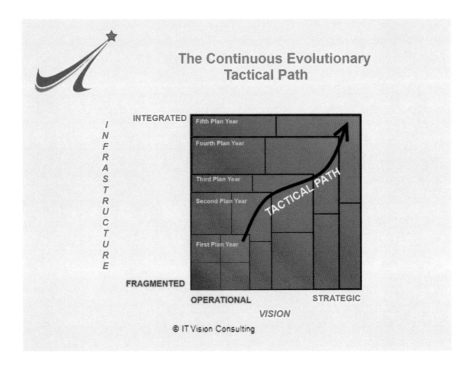

Our goal is to develop a Technology Strategic Target that supports and enhances the Business Strategic Target.

In the first year that you write your plan you might establish a Strategic Target that is five years away. The second plan might be written a couple of years after the initial plan year. The business will have changed a bit and so will technology. So the Strategic Target might move to the right or left by some amount (imagine being at a rifle range), and it will also move a couple of years further into the future (or downrange).

This will happen repeatedly over the years. Let's call the path to the Strategic Target the Tactical Path. If we plan well the Tactical Path will be smooth and evolutionary. Corrections to the Tactical Path will be minimized and so will costs. Conversely, if we don't plan well or with sufficient frequency, the Tactical Path will be riddled with discontinuities and significant technology changes that will increase costs and have a negative effect on enterprise competitiveness.

The Vision And Infrastructure Matrix

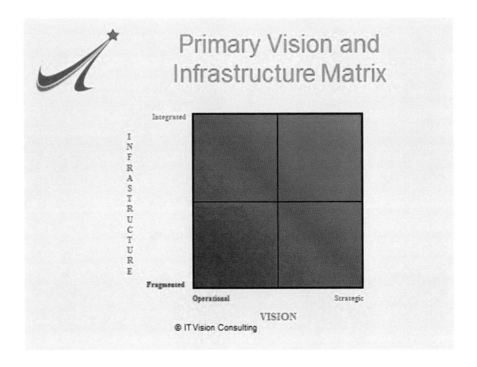

This book is specifically written for the use of information technology teams. It addresses the issue that IT teams work in an incredibly fast-paced, rapidly changing environment. They can easily find themselves a bit segregated from the main business because they are so intensely focused on technology activities. In these pages, you will find specifically tailored guidance to help IT teams integrate with the core enterprise and become great contributors to the enterprise mission.

Throughout this discussion, we will be referring to the Vision and Infrastructure Matrix shown above. We have all seen these types of charts before. The red zone is the area that it is important to move away from. The green area is the goal.

Vision and Infrastructure were chosen as the axes because they are, as I have said before, the most essential, and most basic, elements of strategic planning. To be successful, any enterprise must have a Vision of where it is going. This seems obvious but, as discussed previously, there are many businesses and government agencies that don't have a fully defined and explained Vision Statement that is embedded in the culture of the company and ingrained into the employees.

Whether or not there is a developed and defined Enterprise Vision Statement, there is always an intrinsic Enterprise Infrastructure.

The Infrastructure is the organizational platform on which the enterprise is built. It may have a pyramidal or matrix organizational structure, fully consolidated or distributed offices. All business activities may be completely in-sourced or various mission elements may be handled through one or more contracts, etc. Whether by deliberate design or by circumstance, there is always an Infrastructure. In the best organizations a strong and influential leader has established a clear, concise Vision that becomes the basis for developing the Infrastructure.

In order to ensure coherence with the defined Enterprise Vision it is essential to define clearly and state a Vision for the IT team. There must also be a clearly defined Infrastructure on which the technical systems that support the business are based. This Technical Infrastructure can be a set of protocols, a computing platform and/or a software suite. Whatever the Infrastructure is, it must be built to support and enhance the Vision. The Infrastructure is the framework on which all enterprise applications ride.

21

In terms of sequence, the Vision must first be established, followed by the Infrastructure on which are layered the applications.

Enterprise Vision Is The Driver

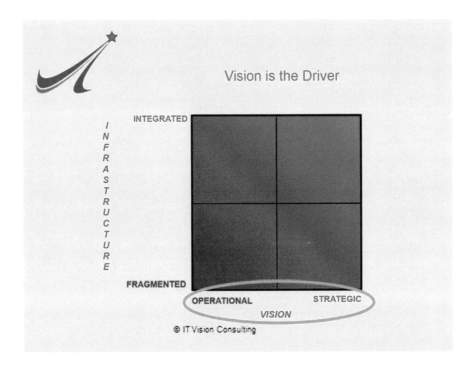

If we were to put the above chart in mathematical terms we would call Enterprise Vision the independent variable which is why I have put it on the traditional "x" axis. It is the independent variable because it is deliberately defined and fixed for the enterprise by the executive team. If it changes it does so only every few years and only through the action of the executive team.

Enterprise Vision ranges from Operational through Strategic.

Operational Vision is what is needed to get through the day-to-day, or short range, tasks of producing product or performing the background actions that support production activities.

Strategic Vision is that clearly defined view of the future that states where the business will be at the end of the planning horizon. In this book, we will be focused on Strategic Vision. However, it is important to acknowledge and include in the planning process the manager who, of necessity, must work with a day-to-day or Operational Vision.

The operational manager is critical to the business. Some who are reading this book may be an operational manager or have held an operations manager position at one time or another. This is the team player who keeps the daily processes running smoothly, ensures that the raw materials (literally and figuratively) arrive on time, get used properly and turned into a product that goes out the door on time with high quality. This is not the person who is responsible for the long-term Vision of the enterprise. However, this is the person who has years of experience that we draw on when determining how to do new things without disrupting production. It could also be a person, depending on the type of company and operational requirements, who will over time move to a position in which they are eventually responsible for the Vision process in a more strategic manner. The person with Operational Vision is a key individual who must be allowed and encouraged to play their operational position on the team and be consulted about how the Strategic Vision affects the ability of their team to do their job.

23

This book is written for the person who is, or who wants to be, the Visionary leader who is depending on others to do their jobs while they perform their task of understanding best where to take the organization. This is the highly paid person who, if they do their job right, makes it possible for the rest of us to keep our jobs. Their ability to envision clearly the future of the marketplace, the competition and the enterprise means the difference between long-term success or failure. Their skill is vital, and their decisions may be of broader consequence than those of most others in the organization. Their ability to put all this information into a concise, clear, energizing, action-oriented Vision Statement can make the difference between organizational success and failure over the long term.

Hopefully, your executive-level business leaders will not be focused on day-to-day or operational issues. For your business to be successful they must have a Strategic Vision. That seems obvious but we have probably all, in both the private and public sector, encountered a surprising number of executives who operate from a task list instead of a long-term Vision. I once worked for a chief executive who kept a list of tasks that he reported on to our board each month. Each of these tasks was a short term accomplishment designed to show how much work he was doing. The rest of us worked with him and for him on those tasks. He never produced a Strategic Vision. The organization of course had not progressed at all while he was there. We got work done but we didn't move forward.

Conversely, the greatest CIO I worked for operated with solely strategic objectives and constantly encouraged us to reach a long-term Vision that he had for the corporate information technology group. That Information Technology Vision supported an equally vivid Enterprise Vision that the corporate CEO consistently and clearly presented to our CIO and the rest of the corporation's top executives. We knew where we

24

were going and how we were going to get there so we accomplished our daily jobs enthusiastically and effectively. Our progress was amazing. The CIO and the CEO played their positions well, and the rest of the team knew clearly what their roles were. We were headed for, and we reached, the green area in the top right corner of the Vision and Infrastructure Matrix.

Technology Vision Is Driven By Strategic Business Vision

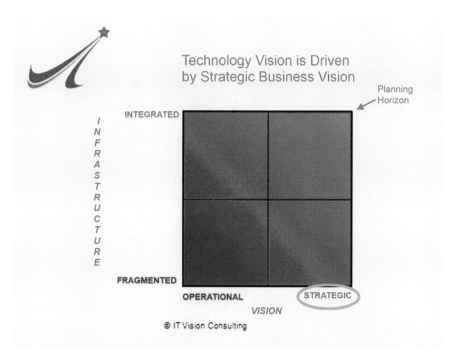

In the context of this book Strategic means a few years into the future. The limit of the Strategic Vision is at the Planning Horizon. How far into the future the planning horizon is depends on the enterprise and the industry the enterprise is in. Typically, it will be about three to five years for the Integrated IT And Business Vision. It could be much longer for some projects and enterprises.

IT Vision in support of corporate planning has two distinct characteristics. It must be long-term and Strategic. It cannot be short-term and Operational. I feel compelled to reemphasize that the IT Vision is dependent upon, and must support, the Business Vision of the organization which, throughout the analysis, is the primary fixed and independent variable.

This all seems obvious. But if it is so obvious, then why do so many IT organizations fail to have a clearly worded IT Strategic Vision that fully supports – and enhances – the Strategic Enterprise Vision?

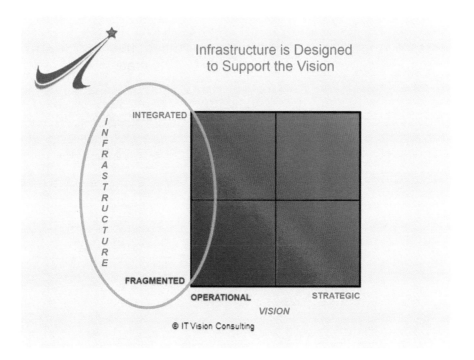

Enterprise and Technical Infrastructures generally run from fragmented to integrated. The overall enterprise may have a structure that is integrated in, or between, some departments or divisions and is fragmented in other areas. In some parts of the enterprise there may be great integration of business flow between divisions while other inter-organizational interactions may be inefficient and jumbled.

I think it is fair to say that the majority of us involved in the strategic planning process must be focused on the goal of reaching the fully Integrated Infrastructure. That's difficult.

27

Few, if any, of us will ever completely reach that goal because the environment is perpetually changing.

For IT people the technology is evolving so rapidly that as soon as we feel like we are getting closer to the goal of organizational and systems integration a new technology emerges that we have to bring coherently into the mix. Then we have to administratively reorganize to support it effectively. As a consequence, we almost surely have some type of Infrastructure fragmentation that we are contending with and constantly working to remove from the system. However, if we don't at least work toward that goal, then we will have a horribly fragmented infrastructure in which costs are high and operational reliability is low.

Technology Infrastructure Is Driven By Strategic Business Infrastructure

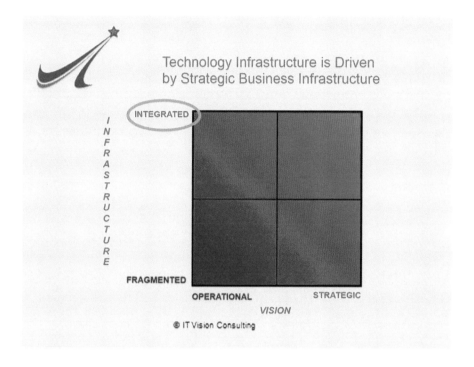

The IT professional is striving for integration across technologies as well as integration with the business structure and processes.

In a way, the job the IT team has to achieve within the technology group is similar to the job the executive team has to accomplish for the business. It will help business development if the IT team understands this. The business executives have to make sure they have a Business Infrastructure that integrates processes from input to output and assures coherence of operation across divisions. The IT

29

professional generally understands the need to integrate across a mass of technologies serving the corporation.

The IT professional with true business appreciation will also understand the integration that has to take place between all the business processes and the technology that supports them.

Technology applications may succeed or fail not just because the technology itself was implemented correctly or incorrectly. The technology can operate beautifully. However, if the technology team doesn't include someone who understands, and has a strong appreciation for, the business processes in some detail the perfectly working technical application will be useless.

On the other hand, the technologists who have taken time to understand fully the business practices and needs of their enterprise customers have a great opportunity to do much more than effectively support them. They have the golden opportunity to enhance the efficiency and effectiveness of the people they are supporting to a degree that enables them to overwhelm the competition and delight their customers.

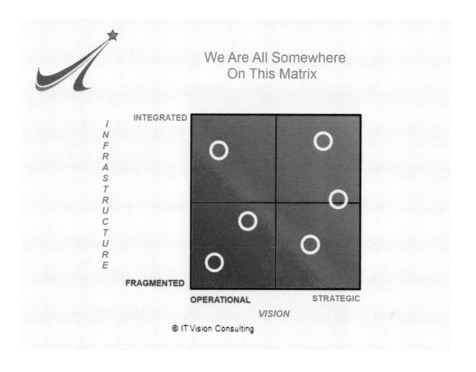

It is safe to say that any organization can be defined as being somewhere on this Vision and Infrastructure matrix.

In the worst case, an organization might be ruled by a leader with a day-to-day operational list of short-term objectives which is, in reality, no Vision at all. Since there is no Vision, there can't be an integrated enterprise Infrastructure that supports that Vision. In fact, the Infrastructure will in all probability be forced into the fragmented zone since there is no Strategic Vision to give it direction and substance. An organization in this red zone of the quadrant is almost surely an organization in trouble and which, at the very best, is providing a disservice to its customers. An organization with only an Operational Vision is virtually guaranteed to be an organization with a fragmented Infrastructure.

In the best case, the chief executive will have a clear Vision of where the organization is going and make that Vision known to all. The strategic chief executive will promote that Vision so well that those responsible for implementing the Vision will make sure that the organization has a well-defined, highly integrated organizational Infrastructure. The team led by this strong Visionary will almost surely create robust internal efficiencies and ensure that raw materials translate to quality products for the customer at minimal cost of operation.

This fortunate enterprise will almost surely have selected an IT executive who creates a Complementary Technology Vision and Infrastructure that help to assure the success of the business objectives. This is the highly successful and extremely competitive organization in the green zone.

The top IT executive's job in this most efficient of organizations is to make sure that the Integrated IT Infrastructure reflects, supports and enhances the Integrated Business Infrastructure. In terms of our earlier discussion, this chief IT executive must make sure all the time that their organization is consciously competent.

This is, in effect, a partnership the CIO enters into with the executive committee on behalf of the IT team. And it is a partnership that is becoming more important as technology becomes a stronger part of our societal and Business Infrastructure. The increasing importance and pervasiveness of a clear IT Vision and Integrated Infrastructure that enhance enterprise performance is the reason the CIO position was brought into existence. This is why in most highly successful organizations the CIO and/or the CTO work directly for the chief executive.

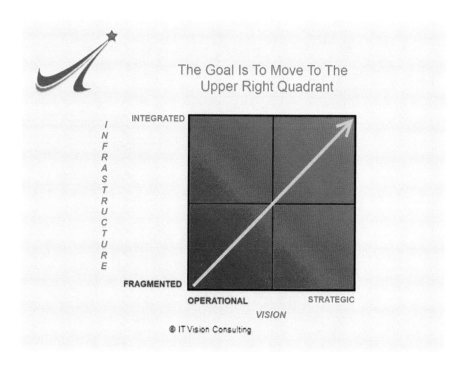

None of this is easy stuff. However, the consistent and persistent goal must constantly be to drive the organization away from the red zone and into the green zone of the upper-right quadrant.

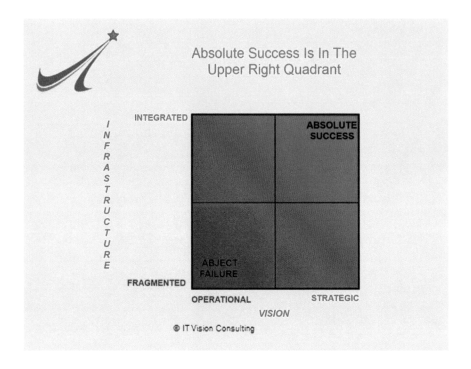

The organization in the bottom left red zone is doomed to abject failure caused by unclear objectives and organizational inefficiencies. Those who achieve the upper right green zone will almost surely dominate their industry and achieve absolute success.

34

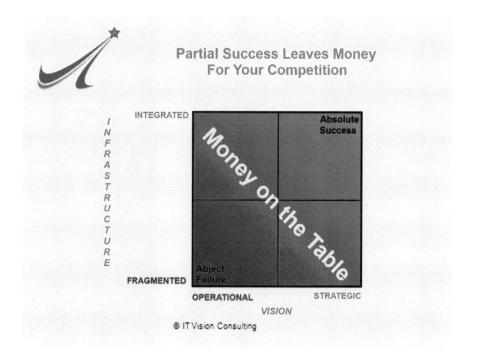

Most organization operate somewhere in the orange zone for many reasons; some valid and some not valid at all. The business and/or technology leadership may not have the skill, knowledge or experience to clearly see or define a Strategic Vision. While most leaders have a Vision that lies beyond operational it may fall somewhat short and be in an area that, for convenience, we can call tactical.

We have already stated that when speaking of Vision and Infrastructure it makes sense to define Vision as the independent variable and Infrastructure as the dependent variable. It is the Vision for the organization that defines what the Infrastructure of the organization will be. A clearly stated and well-advertised Strategic Vision has a better chance of resulting in a fully Integrated Infrastructure. Nevertheless, in the real world, organizational Infrastructures may be more or less compartmented. Not totally fragmented, but not fully integrated either. Most of our organizational and Technical Infrastructures are more or less compartmentalized because of business or technical evolution or any number of other valid or invalid reasons.

Wherever we are in this region between abject failure and absolute success we are leaving money on the table because of excess cost or inability to reach our full market potential. Most enterprises operate somewhere in this orange region. Obviously, the closer to the upper-right corner we are the more effective and efficient we will be.

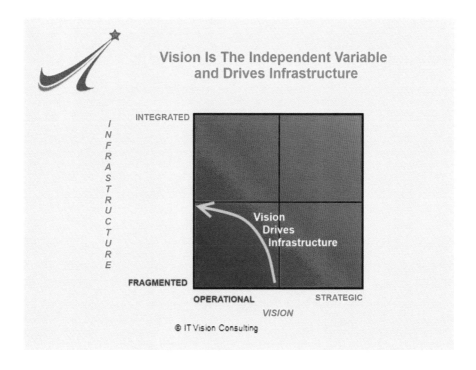

So, Business Vision is the originator and driver of everything. Without a Business Vision the process can't even begin and the business is doomed to mediocrity at best and perhaps even failure. For some, a valid Strategic Business Vision may be no more than three years in the future. For others, like President Kennedy, it is a nine year goal stated on May 25th, 1961 of "before this decade is out of landing a man on the moon and returning him safely to earth". For still others it is approximately a 70 year long project leading toward the creation of economical fusion power. How far into the future the Vision is depends on the needs of the business and the ability of the business executives. Whatever the Vision is, it has to be concise, straightforward and inspirational. That's not simple to do but it is perhaps where executives best earn their money.

Leadership Is Everything

We talked earlier about the Chief Executive who worked from a task list. He was very effective at getting his list of tasks accomplished, and his reports to the board were well received because he got a lot done. However, he never established a Strategic Vision or encouraged the development of an Integrated Infrastructure. Unhappily, he also wasn't a very effective manager. All of this was hidden from the board because he overwhelmed them with information about day-to-day activities that he accomplished himself. Needless to say, the board was inexperienced and not very demanding. This Chief Executive was an excellent administrator in a leadership position. The organization had a mission with great potential. However, it never moved out of the red zone on the Vision Infrastructure Matrix.

We all have great skills of some kind. In the context of this discussion, people are strong leaders, strong managers or strong administrators. We need all three in the organization, but we will never find large amounts of all three in the same person.

Experience shows that an excellent leader will be a good manager but have left any strong administrative skills behind a long time ago. They will also have little interest left for administration. That is why superior leaders almost always have an administrative assistant working for them. An outstanding manager will have some amount of leadership and administrative skills. A strong administrator may also have some amount of management skill but have little leadership skill. The skill set for each of us may shift as our career progresses but a person won't have strong skills in all three areas at the same time.

Strong leaders move us to the green zone because they are almost certain to establish a clear Strategic Vision and encourage the development of an Integrated Infrastructure. These excellent leaders have probably created an environment in which they have a strong management team that leads those responsible for administering the operational system.

All three skills are necessary in the organization as a whole. We want the person in the chief executive position to be fully focused on leadership. An excellent executive in the top leadership position will make sure they have a strong management team focused on managing people, processes and systems. If a top executive has to spend a lot of time on management then there should be, and probably will be, a staff change.

The lesson of leadership is one that I had the great fortune to learn early in my career. I'm going to disguise the following story a bit so that it doesn't give too much away about the organization and people involved.

I once worked for an enterprise with a headquarters function of about 600 people and 10 very important remote offices with 5 to 30 highly skilled people at each location. To make a long story short our organization had just received an extremely bad business rating and our chief executive, who happened to be my direct boss, was fired.

A new chief executive was brought in from outside. I was the most junior member on his staff, but my team had received the highest rating from the reviewing group. Much to my dismay the new chief executive appointed me to the unpleasant task of forming a small team to do our own internal review of the entire organization and recommend strong actions to quickly improve our performance. This was a full time six-month assignment that put my team and me on the road to every remote office.

During those six months I learned the most important lesson in my career about leadership! As we traveled around I found out that the locations that were top performers had the best leaders. Without exception, the performance of the organization directly reflected the performance of the top executive. If the top executive was mediocre or poor the performance of the organization reflected the performance of the top executive even if the rest of the people were excellent and highly motivated. These top leaders provided, and were the only ones who could provide, Vision and the team motivation and desire to create an Infrastructure to achieve that Vision.

This was a startling lesson that I frankly had trouble absorbing. Once I finally understood and accepted this lesson, I was able to report to my very seasoned boss a clear resolution to our organizational problem. Naturally, he already understood this. He just needed good data on where and who the problems were. Some key leadership replacements were made, and the next report from the reviewing team was the best the organization had ever received.

Excellent leaders create excellent organizations.

The lesson was clear. Excellent leaders create excellent organizations. They understand that people will meet the expectations of their leader – low or high. These leaders provide a Vision that excites the team to action and gives them clear objectives.

Excellent leaders minimally manage and they don't administer at all! Leaders know that if they assume a management role rather than an executive role then the people who work for them will expect to be managed, and they will act as if they

41

should be managed. Leaders know that if they unnecessarily take on administrative tasks they won't be in the proper frame of mind to lead. Excellent leaders stay in their leadership roll all the time!

As I worked through this lesson over the years, and as I studied people in leadership positions, I put together the triangle shown below. I believe that all of us have great strength at just on point on this triangle, moderate strength at a second point and no strength at a third point. The normal progression is from administrator to manager to executive leader stopping at some point along the way determined by our interest and skills.

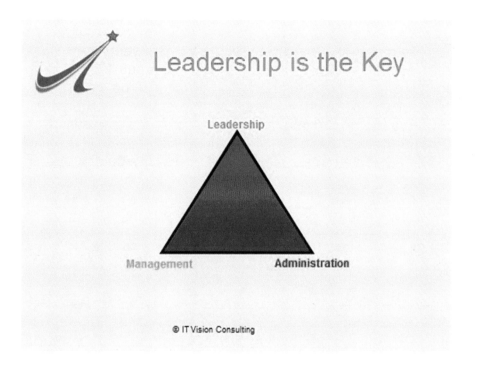

I don't want to belabor this point, but I feel it is important to spend a few more paragraphs on this subject.

I have been fortunate throughout my career to work for many outstanding leaders. Naturally, I've also encountered a few who were much less than notable. The outstanding ones helped me to personally navigate and evolve through this administrator, manager, leader triangle.

In my first two management assignments, I was responsible for small teams of people with heavy administrative duties. My inclination was to set myself up as the most knowledgeable administrator.

Our file systems were perfect and our attention to detail was impeccable. I diligently reviewed every file and all activities to ensure that everything was administratively correct. Nothing escaped my attention. My boss, who was an excellent leader, encouraged me to personally give up these administrative duties and hand them off to others so I could take on more of an organizational management role. When it was clear to him that I didn't understand how to respond to his guidance, he gave me so many cross-functional management assignments that I didn't have any time for micro-administration. I was surprised to learn that without my close administrative attention, things ran better and people were happier. I had made the mistake of administering in a management role.

An organizational transfer put me in a new assignment with huge management and planning responsibilities at a young age. The team I was leading was a bit larger, and they were very good at what they did. I had such a diversity of responsibilities that I hardly knew where to begin. I had already learned not to be a micro-administrator, but I didn't understand what management really was. Instead of being a team manager and excellent staff member I dove into being a prodigious worker. I became a member of my team instead of the leader of my team.

Delegate to the limit of your own guilt and

everyone else's pain.

Happily, one of the highly experienced people working for me as a staff member, and very senior in years and experience, saw the error of my ways. From him, I learned the value and art of delegation and the necessity to step away from work in order to be an effective manager. Once again, this was a difficult lesson for me to absorb, but when I finally did the team operated more efficiently, and I became a better executive staff member making a contribution to organizational efficiency and evolution.

I developed a rule to keep myself in this management role and not slip back into being a member of the team I was supposed to be managing. The rule I still live by is "Delegate to the limit of your own guilt and everyone else's pain". Naturally, this rule is a bit of an exaggeration, but it was what I needed to make sure I played my proper position on the enterprise team.

Years later I found myself in the executive ranks sometimes leading small teams at headquarters locations or very large teams with many layers of management and hundreds of people. In preparation for these roles, I had been well coached by a number of excellent executives who taught me that, at senior levels, it is necessary to lead through influence, not authority. This is a quiet, effective method of executive leadership that allows organizations to operate efficiently in a calm environment.

Learning to lead through influence also gives a person at the "C" level the opportunity and the time to establish and promote a Vision for the organization that increases efficiency.

The Details of The Process

Relationship Of Vision And Infrastructure

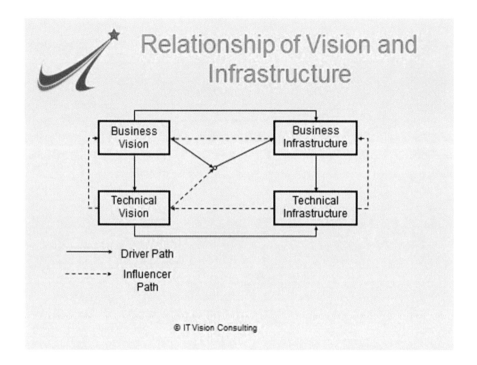

The discussion so far has focused on the relationship between Vision and Infrastructure and the critical necessity for strong leadership when creating a Vision and establishing an Infrastructure. We know it is necessary to ensure that the CIO's team establishes a Technology Vision and Infrastructure that supports, and preferably enhances, the Enterprise Vision and Infrastructure.

46

From this point onward, we will move from discussion of theory into application of the process. We will develop the slide shown above as a mechanism for explaining the process. As we walk through this, we will be discussing the involved relationship between core business and the supporting information technology with respect to Vision and Infrastructure.

Since Business Vision is the independent variable and the originator and driver of everything, we will start with the Business Vision.

The Primary Driver Is The Business Vision

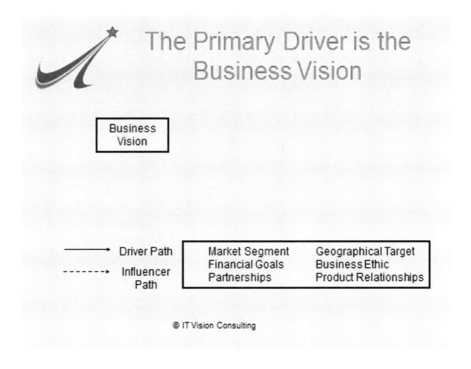

There are clearly a number of high level elements that come together when creating the Business Vision statement. The CEO and the executive team have to make decisions on a number of things that give some practical definition to the Business Vision.

The market has to be narrowed down to some segment of seven continents and six billion people. Financial goals have to be realistically established that support the business's ability to competitively deliver a quality product to market. A business ethic has to be established that employees can be proud of and adheres to the laws and customs of the countries in which the company is selling and setting up offices. Vendor partnerships might have to be established that optimize cash flow and productivity. There may be considerations in a very large corporation of internal product relationships as well as external product relationships. The list is much longer than the few examples shown here.

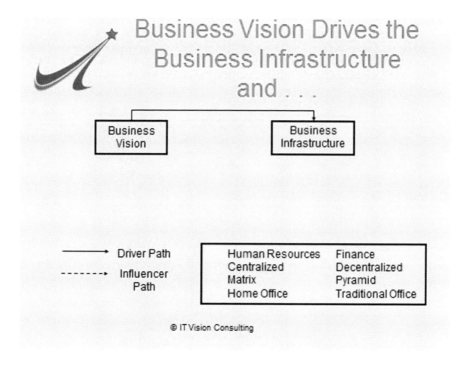

While the Business Vision is being developed, the CEO's entire executive team is, in all probability, examining the Business Infrastructure to see how it has to be revised and improved to support the Business Vision.

Since the CIO is part of the executive team, discussions are sure to arise that result in some amount of influence of information technology on elements of the Business Infrastructure. We will get to that in a couple of slides.

49

Business Vision drives Business Infrastructure. The market and business ethic will drive the structure of the human resources team. The finance departments will have to be organized to reflect the tax structures, pay processes, etc. of the countries in which the organization does business. Various elements of the business may be centralized while others may logically operate better if decentralized. Some business units may be organized along a matrix structure while others may be pyramidal. The organization may be best served with home offices rather than offices centralized in the business district. Or, there may be some mix of home and centralized offices.

The CIO will have to take back to their technology team key points of this discussion that will point the way toward activities and systems that the IT group must put in place, or adjust, to meet the evolving Infrastructure requirements.

Organizations that don't group their information technology systems under a single CIO are at a significant disadvantage because they have no central leader to consolidate this information for them and ensure that the right translation is made between the business language in the executive committee discussions and the technical management teams.

This is the reason the CIO position became more prevalent in the 1980s. Before that, the business leaders had no one person who could ensure that coherent technical systems were in place to support the Business Vision and Infrastructure. Efficiency and effectiveness both suffered.

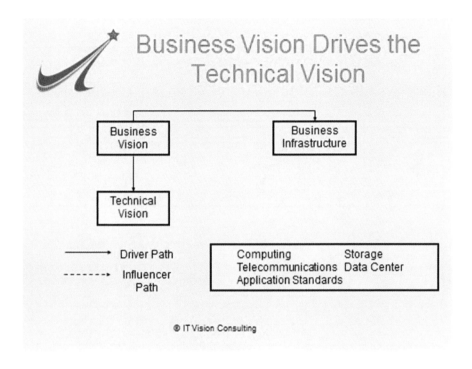

The CIO and their team have to respond to the Business Vision with a Technical Vision that supports that Business Vision. At first blush, or for some, it might seem that all that is needed is a one-sided response to the needs of the business. The executive business leaders state what they need, and the technologists put on their white coats and perform their laboratory magic. In addition to some decisions about which technologies to employ the CIO's team might look at organizational restructuring within the technical ranks so that they stay aligned with the enterprise organizational structure. This, of course, works to some degree. However, this isn't really a Technical Vision. It is only a technology response to a stated business direction.

Feedback Enhances The Business Vision

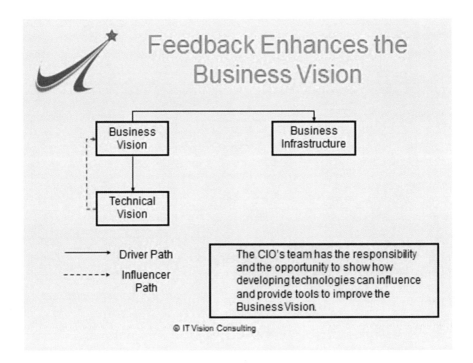

The real value is provided when a truly outstanding CIO and IT team return to the CEO with a Technical Vision that enhances and influences the Business Vision. The CIO who performs in this role may (or may not) have a strong technology background. Most importantly, the CIO has assumed the necessary role of an executive who is a businessperson first and technologist second.

Frankly, the best CIO, and the greatest leader, I ever worked for had very little technology background.

The better the CIO represents their team in a business and leadership role the better chance they have to gain credibility for their team and become embedded within the business processes. This leadership enables the CIO to create a feedback loop between their team and the business. This feedback loop makes the Business Vision more achievable, stronger, and more innovative. It drives the Business Vision toward something of greater strategic value.

This type of CIO isn't just responding with an information technology operations solution. They are responding with a complementary and supportive information Technology Vision with strategic components that fully support the Business Vision. It is a response containing elements that show how IT can enhance the Business Vision, make it more achievable, or provide new opportunities that would not have been recognized without this feedback.

Such a CIO has achieved two important goals in one action. They have led their team to create a strategic IT Vision while integrating the IT Vision with the Business Vision. The executive business leaders will recognize that they have an information technology asset that makes a difference in their ability to compete, become more efficient and effective, improve their standing in the industry and earn more money for the executives, employees and stockholders. As time goes on it will become standard within that enterprise to include Technical Vision as an intrinsic component of the Business Vision.

Business Infrastructure Is Enhanced By Vision Adjustments

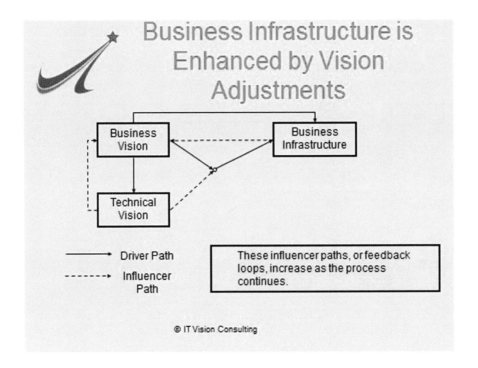

Through this process, the Technical Vision also influences the Business Infrastructure which, of course, has its own feedback loop to adjust the Business Vision.

This feedback process could go on indefinitely, but the executive team will have to be wise enough to call a halt when the process reaches the point of diminishing returns. In the end, the core element and the independent variable remains the Business Vision. Everything else is a dependent variable supporting and enhancing the Business Vision.

54

Technical Infrastructure Is Driven By Technical Vision And Business Infrastructure

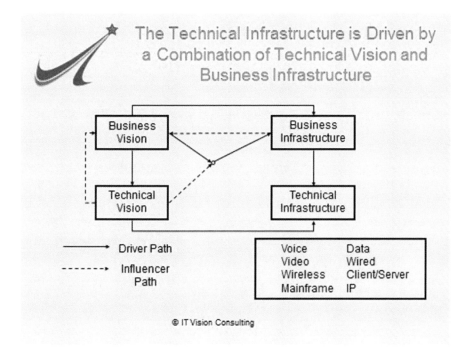

The Technical Infrastructure is Driven by a Combination of Technical Vision and Business Infrastructure

© IT Vision Consulting

In the end (for purposes of this discussion) the CIO's team must develop a Technical Infrastructure that supports the Business Infrastructure and the overall Vision. Again, the technical team may develop Infrastructure elements that influence and enhance the Business Infrastructure and the all-inclusive Vision.

All of this drives the CIO team to have to make highly difficult decisions about the Technical Infrastructure that is required to support the evolving Business Infrastructure. Technology is an extremely expensive part of the business. Costs can only be

55

contained while effectively supporting the enterprise if the various elements of the Infrastructure are well integrated with each other and with the enterprise.

Let me give an example from my own personal experience that illustrates the importance of the IT Infrastructure that is becoming increasingly critical to all enterprises.

About 15 years into my career, I went to work as director of voice and data network services for an up and coming on-line services company. The business growth rate was 40% per year, and the network growth rate was 100% per year because of the evolving distribution of customers. I was there only about four months when the network became dramatically overloaded by a seasonal training surge. Training classes had to be rescheduled or canceled. The training and sales staffs were angry. C revenue was being lost. Future revenue was in great danger, and it was embarrassing. No one warned me about the dramatic extent of this seasonal traffic. Some of this was just poor planning and communication between the marketing, sales and technical staffs. Some of it, I soon realized, was a devious recognition by the computer staff that their systems would not be able to handle the load, and it would be better for them if the network failed instead of the computing systems. So, the network became the choke point, and I was ready to choke myself to end my misery. I was sure I was going to be fired.

Once we got through the seasonal mess, I had a long discussion with my VP about the situation. He told me this happened every year, and that we could never predict the size or source of the seasonal traffic that was going to come through the network. I told him that was unacceptable, and I went to work to find the expert who understood the Business Vision and the marketing and sales plan. I took this path in part because of professional pride. I also didn't want to go through this agony and embarrassment every year.

I found the guru I was looking for in the finance department. All strategic planning for the corporation ended up funneling through him because he had to have that information to develop the multi-year financial plan.

I'll make a very long, arduous and involved story short. Armed with the Business Infrastructure and Vision information he provided to me, I made sure the network was of sufficient size in the right locations to handle the seasonal load every year that I was there. I used the knowledge of the Business Vision and Infrastructure to establish the correct human Infrastructure for my team and make changes in the network Infrastructure that actually reduced unit costs of operation while adding the flexibility needed to support the rapidly evolving market. However, much more than that I began a close relationship with the marketing and sales teams that helped them generate more revenue and reduce overall enterprise costs by selling in areas where it cost less to establish large network channels. The network technology wasn't just supporting the mission; it was actually adding value to the mission!

The Strategic Vision

Developing The Strategic Vision

Developing the Strategic Vision

- The Business Vision is the Independent Variable developed by the business leaders
- The Technical Vision depends on:
  - The general direction of the technology industry
  - The relationship of technology elements across the industry
  - The selection of technology elements that support and enhance the Business Vision

© IT Vision Consulting

We have talked about and emphasized repeatedly that the Business Vision is the starting point of all of our analysis and is the independent variable. This independent variable receives some feedback and adjustment throughout the process we are discussing. However, once set, it is the guiding point for all that we do.

While the Technical Vision supports and enhances the Business Vision it is guided by the general direction of the

58

technology industry and the relationship of the technology elements across that industry. IT people who have to figure this stuff out are pretty well rewarded if they do this job skillfully. They should be because this is complex stuff that involves a large number of variables in quickly evolving technology segments.

Technology Without Business Application Has No Value!

The Technical Infrastructure
Exists Solely to Support the
Business Infrastructure
Because
Technology Without Business
Application Has No Value!

® IT Vision Consulting

In the midst of this decision process, all members of the technology team have to discipline themselves to resist the temptation to include certain elements of technology just because they are so cool! And technology is cool! That's why it sells so well to the mainstream population. However, technology is also expensive, and buying bits and pieces here and there because of its coolness can result in a lot of wasted dollars for the corporation and detract from reaching the upper-right corner of our Vision and Infrastructure matrix. Every member of the technology team has to remember that the Technical Infrastructure exists solely to support the Business Infrastructure because technology without business application has no value.

I recently worked for a technology organization that did good work for its customers. The people were highly dedicated and enjoyed their work. Their customers were moderately happy. The Vision and Infrastructure from an organizational perspective were clear. The issue was that the technologists and the executive leadership weren't fully in synch with each other. The leadership thought the technology people were going the right way, but the reality was that the technology team was more dedicated to their enjoyment of the technology than they were to the accomplishment of the mission. Consequently, technology costs were higher than they should have been and this was the reason the customers were only moderately happy. The cost of the technology was high, but the value of the technology was low in comparison.

The task was clear. We needed to define a Technology Vision that was exciting to the already highly dedicated technology team and that was in synch with the Enterprise Vision. Beyond that, we needed to develop an Infrastructure that more closely supported that Vision without damaging the morale of a very enthusiastic group of technologists.

Because this enterprise was an information technology group, I defined the Vision as a stronger Information Service Tool which would bring a higher level of customer satisfaction to moderately happy customers. The Infrastructure reflected the Vision and contained Action Items that were required to build the Infrastructure, achieve the Vision and make our customer's happier.

Since technologists understand and respond to charts the Vision, Infrastructure and Strategic Target were outlined in the type of chart we are discussing in this book. We defined the long term dangers of staying in the red zone and the benefits to the individuals, the organization and our customers of moving to the green zone. This was admittedly a sales pitch to the technology team, but they had to believe in the Vision and embrace it whole heartedly if we were going to achieve it. It worked. Technology cost of operation decreased over time and customer satisfaction increased dramatically!

Cost, Price and Value

Cost, Price and Value

- Cost of acquisition plus cost of operation of technology must help keep enterprise cost of operation as low as possible
- Keeping total cost of ownership low helps improve organizational margins and price competitiveness
- Excellent Infrastructure focused on the Vision helps make Value to the customer higher than the Price of the product

® IT Vision Consulting

Everything has a cost to manufacture or purchase. If enterprises are to be competitive in the marketplace, their costs must be kept as low as possible to maximize the enterprise's margins. The technology team with a close eye on the organization's Vision and Infrastructure goals will understand their obligation to keep costs contained while assuring the use of high-quality systems to produce great customer satisfaction. More importantly, that technology team will be making cost of acquisition and cost of ownership decisions that have business value as a higher priority than technological "coolness".

62

The Strategic Target Intersection

- A effective Strategic Vision results when the Technical Vision supports and enhances the Business Vision
- The Technical Infrastructure elements must be Integrated with each other and with the Business Infrastructure elements
- The intersection of the Integrated Infrastructure and the Strategic Vision is the Strategic Target

® IT Vision Consulting

All of this discussion to this point reduces to these three statements.

- An effective Strategic Vision results when the Technical Vision supports and enhances the Business Vision.
- The Technical Infrastructure elements must be integrated with each other and with the Business Infrastructure elements.
- The intersection of the Integrated Infrastructure and the Strategic Vision is the Strategic Target.

63

The Strategic Target

This Planning Process Results In A Strategic Target

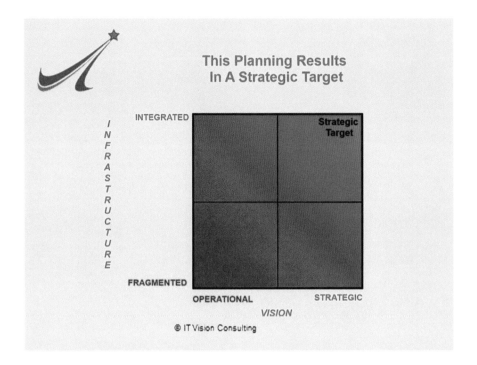

The region of our matrix that results in Absolute Success is the Strategic Target. The Strategic Target is the intersection of a clearly stated Strategic Vision and a well implemented Integrated Infrastructure.

Choosing the technology component of the Strategic Target is especially challenging for the IT professional. There are many interrelated components of IT with each one of them evolving at a different rate and oftentimes in unexpected ways. For example, a strategic planner in the early 1990s might have totally missed the huge positive effect the Internet would have by the late 1990s. Most IT people at that time who were focused on network evolution were arguing the merits of X.25 versus SNA, both of which faded to insignificance with the advent of the Internet Protocol. In the period of less than a decade network planning changed dramatically.

Segregated networks each handling voice, video or data were commonplace even in the mid-1990s with many predicting that full network integration might not occur until a couple of decades into the 21st century. However, early in that first decade of the new century IP voice, data and video were fully integrated in the same network switches, desktop processors and transmission systems.

There is some similarity to the astronomer who is trying to choose the right lens when looking at an object in space. A very high-powered lens would produce the desired image of a distant star. However, such a high-powered lens might make the star extremely hard to find because the field of view is so narrow. Just a small angle of maladjustment can have the astronomer pulling their hair out as they try to bring the telescope to precisely the right altitude and azimuth to find the star. However, moving to a less powerful lens will bring the star into the larger field of view fairly quickly.

The strategic planner has to be sufficiently experienced to understand what the proper amount of granularity is when choosing the detail with which to describe the Strategic Target and also how far into the future the target should be placed.

Placing the Strategic Target too far in the future can have a very misleading result.

The above picture was published by the Rand Corporation in the mid-twentieth century. It illustrates the hazards of choosing the technology component of a Strategic Target. It is certainly not meant to be critical of the Rand Corporation which in the early 1950s projected what a home computer would look like in 2004. The picture makes it clear that Rand Corporation missed the mark badly. However, they never had a chance of hitting the mark! The pace of technology in the early 1950s and before was dramatically slower than it was in the last half of the 20th century. Few, if any, of the scientists foresaw the invention of the transistor, the large-scale integrated circuit, the inventions that would come out of the space program, or the effect of Moore's Law and other technology "laws".

Some of the "laws" concerning technology evolution that have evolved over the last few decades give us what seems to be a pretty accurate picture of the direction in which technology is going. If these "laws" had been understood at the time that the Rand Corporation made their home computer prediction it would be interesting to see how close to the mark they might have been. The following two charts give just a couple of examples of the dramatic pace of Information Technology evolution.

Many information technologists are familiar with Gordon Moore's Law which was proposed in 1965 and which has had a few different formulations and interpretations over time. In summary, the thrust of this law is that computing chips will see a doubling of real processor power every two years on average. In retrospect this has been pretty accurate. One measure reveals that there has been a doubling of real computing power every 2.3 years, on average, since the birth of modern computing.

Then there are the other "laws" which affect our view of the IT future.

- Kryder's Law states that density of information on digital storage devices has been doubling every 23 months, on average, since 1956.
- George Gilder originally observed in the 1980s that "bandwidth grows at least three times faster than computer power".
- Martin Cooper noted that the spectrum efficiency of radio communication (both voice and data) has doubled

every two and a half years, over 104 years, since radio waves were first used for communication.

- Nishimura's Law can be interpreted to say that video display size available at the same cost doubles every 3.6 years.

I could go on, but the point is made that the Technical Vision is dependent upon some very fast changing basic elements of our environment.

Another point is that inventions along each of these fast-moving development tracks work to influence each other and combine to allow engineers to create new technology inventions at prodigious rates. Happily, we have these proven "laws" and can anticipate the general direction and rate of change of technology. For example,

- if you knew from the Business Vision and Infrastructure that your business needed very high bandwidth between two locations, and
- you knew that the bandwidth requirements would double every two years, and
- you expected a long lifetime for your system, and
- it was already operating at 10s of Megabits per second,

then you might choose a wired (fiber) transmission system over a wireless (microwave) transmission system.

Your technology response depends on both the needs of the business as well as the anticipated evolution of the types of technologies available.

Given this and other information, we might predict that today's $3,000 desktop computer will in the year 2020 cost 1/500th of what it costs today, weigh no more than a cell phone, and be able to communicate wirelessly from many locations at a rate adequate to handle **today's** applications. Since application

68

bandwidth requirements are evolving faster than wide area wireless bandwidth transmission capability there will probably still be a need to reach the rest of the world through a wired backbone accessed by regional or local wireless access points.

Today's $3,000 Desktop Computer

- In 1986:
  - Would have cost $25,000
  - Been the size of your desk
  - Equivalent broadband network connection would have been $2,000 per month to limited locations
- In 2020
  - Will cost about $6 for the same computing power
  - Will fit in your pocket
  - Will connect wirelessly from most locations at a speed faster than today's wired connection for the same cost.

© IT Vision Consulting

Happily, almost all of us involved in strategic planning don't have to worry about planning 10 years or more into the future. Our planning horizon is generally shorter. However, the pace of evolution described by the technology evolution "laws" reveals that IT development might very well be evolving at a much faster pace than the organization you may be supporting.

The Tactical Path

Tactical Path

Tactical Path

Gets us from where we are today to the Strategic Target in the most efficient and effective manner possible

© IT Vision Consulting

The Tactical Path is where the incremental planning takes place. It is through the process of building this path that each of the technical elements is integrated with each other and with the business to lead us to the Strategic Target in the most efficient method possible.

70

Once we have established the Strategic Target, we know two points along this path. With total certainty, we know where we are today. By convention, we know the point on the path that is the Strategic Target because we have defined it as an intersection of Vision and Infrastructure at some future date we have chosen.

As business people, we know the logical and sequential steps we have to take each calendar quarter or year to take the business from where we are to the Strategic Target.

The technologists on the CIO's team know the same things with respect to Information Technology and Systems.

We can use this interrelated set of steps to define the path to the Strategic Target we establish. It is periodically necessary to reevaluate the plan during a new planning year, at which point we go through the entire process again to set a fresh Strategic Target at some extended future date. This fresh plan is like a mid-course correction for a space shot.

Integrated Planning Results In A Strategic Target

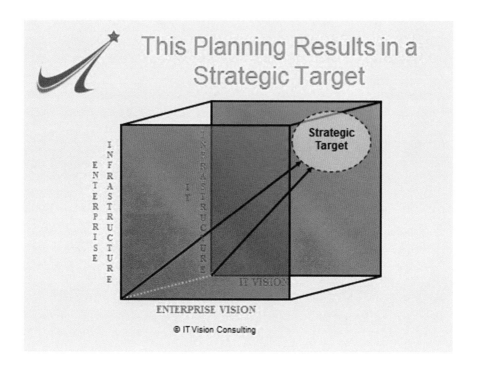

This Planning Results in a Strategic Target

ENTERPRISE VISION

® IT Vision Consulting

The Strategic Target Moves!

Over time, the Business Vision will change because all kinds of other things like leadership, the market, the economy, technology, and culture change. Disasters happen that modify any or all of these elements to eliminate, change or create markets. Fresh discoveries in the business or technology segment may open new possibilities and change the conduct of business. The Strategic Target will periodically move into the future by the same interval as the planning cycle.

Figuratively, the target may also move slightly side to side in our sights as different elements of the Strategic Target are revised.

The Strategic Target Moves For All Kinds Of Good Reasons

The Strategic Target Moves!

- Business Vision Changes
- Leadership Changes
- The Market Changes
- The Economy Changes
- Technology Changes
- Culture Evolves
- Disasters Happen
- Breakthroughs Happen

© IT Vision Consulting

The process described in this book helps anchor the Strategic Target so that it isn't subject to movement through whim or minor changes in the environment. By anchoring the Strategic Target in a clearly stated and carefully thought out Strategic Vision and an Integrated Infrastructure there is increased certainty that the Strategic Target will remain relatively consistent. Except for very major events (disasters or near disasters) inside or outside the enterprise the process described here should be one that everyone in the enterprise can count on. It is a proven method for developing a smooth, evolutionary Tactical Path to reach the Strategic Target on the planning horizon which should be three to five years in the future.

The Path To The Strategic Target Changes

The Path to the Strategic Target Changes

But if we plan effectively!

- The path avoids discontinuities that create excess cost
- The path incorporates timely mid course corrections that optimize operating efficiency
- It becomes more linear than non-linear
- It is evolutionary rather than revolutionary

© IT Vision Consulting

For a variety of good reasons the Strategic Target does move a bit. However, if we plan with wisely chosen frequency, we can develop a path to this moving target that avoids the sharp turns and discontinuities that result in excess costs. Just as is true with a space mission to a distant planet, we can employ timely mid-course corrections that permit us to reach our destination with minimal cost to the business and in a manner that fully supports the business objectives. It is, in effect, a continuous improvement process applied to strategic planning.

It is important to remember that what the IT team is really doing during this planning process is discovering the requirements for construction of an Infrastructure. What type of, or what mix of, computing platforms is needed? Should the phone system be integrated with the data system or should their control systems be geographically separated to improve the survivability of the business operation? What is the standard for and what is the evolutionary path of the client/server systems? Or, will there even be a company owned and operated client/server system? The decisions about what applications will ride on the Infrastructure come later and are not part of the planning process at this stage.

I worked for a short time for a business executive who kept asking for specific applications to support the business we were in. He never told us what the business direction was and kept putting off our suggestions for investment in an ongoing, coherent Infrastructure. As he asked for applications I would tell him how much that application would cost. That cost, of course, was higher than necessary because it wasn't going to be built on an Integrated Infrastructure guided by a clear Strategic Vision. Operational costs were increasing, and many applications couldn't be afforded because we would have had to put in place a fragmented Infrastructure that added to the application cost. He was confused and frustrated. The rest of us were exasperated and angry, and we weren't making much progress considering the effort we were expending. We were stuck in abysmal failure in the lower left portion of our Vision/Infrastructure matrix. That executive finally left.

75

Our problem was that there was no Business Vision on which to base any kind of Infrastructure. It is like a major corporation putting interstate truck terminals 1,000 miles away from each other with the only Infrastructure between them being two-lane roads that can carry no more than the weight of a small horse trailer. The truck terminals might be state of the art and the trucks shiny new vehicles with excellently trained drivers. However, they are useless to the business because there is no transportation Infrastructure.

The Continuous, Evolutionary Tactical Path

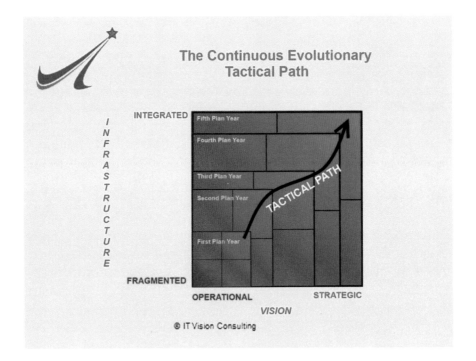

If we plan with sufficient frequency and thoroughness, the Tactical Path will have minimal mid-course corrections. A Tactical Path that weaves wildly back and forth is one reflecting a poorly defined Vision or a Vision revisited without enough frequency. This is not to say that the Vision has to be redefined in each planning cycle. In fact, an excellent Vision may remain the same over multiple planning cycles and only be revised when it has been almost fully attained. Any new Strategic Vision will, in all probability, build on the successes of the previous Strategic Visions.

A Tactical Path with major deviations may also reflect an insufficiently Integrated Infrastructure or an Infrastructure that does not effectively support the Vision. However, if we do our planning process properly we will find ourselves on a close to linear evolutionary Tactical Path without the discontinuities that result in excessive costs and impaired competitive position.

The One Page Guiding Document

Target, Benefits and Actions

Target, Benefits, Actions

- Target – We will work as a team to move our systems and products:
  - From . . . to . . ..
  - From . . . to . . ..
- Benefits – Our technical products and services:
  - Will provide . . ..
  - Will be . . ..
- Actions – As a team we will take these Actions to reach this Target and achieve these Benefits:

© IT Vision Consulting

Keep it simple because it will get complicated all by itself.

When you are working to reach a Target you are essentially moving from one place to another place. The only reason for an enterprise to move to that Target is that there is some business Benefit in doing so. Obviously, to reach the Target and achieve those Benefits some Actions have to be taken. All of this brings us to a point that I like to constantly remind people of. It is important to keep things simple because they will get complicated all by themselves! This book reflects strong adherence to that principle.

Once all the work described in the previous pages of this book has been accomplished a one-page document can be published that summarizes where the chief technology executive is taking the team.

An **example** of this document is shown on the next page.

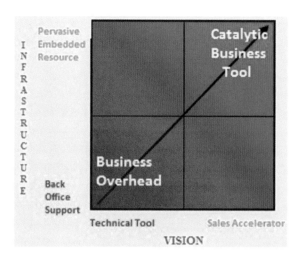

TARGET – We will work as a team to move our systems and products:

- From Business Overhead Elements to Catalytic Business Tools
- From Discrete Technical Tools to Sales Acceleration Systems
- From Back Office Support Elements to an Essential Resource that Pervades Every Part of the Enterprise
- Etc.

BENEFITS - Our technical products and services:

- Will provide . . ..
- Will be . . ..
- Etc.

ACTIONS - As a team we will take these Actions to reach this Target and achieve these Benefits:

- Leverage . . ..
- Provide . . ..
- Implement . . ..
- Etc.

80

When it is completed everyone should be given a copy, and it should be placed on the wall as a large poster that is in full view of the entire team. This **example** contains a matrix at the top of the page that describes:

- where the technology team is today on the Vision and Infrastructure axes,
- where it must be on these axes at the end of the planning horizon,
- the operational service the team provides today, and
- the Strategic Target service it is expected to provide at the end of the planning horizon.

The sample message delivered within the matrix is clear. "We will move our technology systems from being a business overhead function to a catalytic business tool."

Underneath this matrix is a bullet point description of:

- the Strategic Target or Vision,
- the Benefits that accrue for the enterprise, and
- the Actions that must be taken to achieve those Benefits.

This one-page chart tells the IT team what they need to do. It also tells everyone in the enterprise, in clear business terms, how and why the IT team is engaged in the continuing set of actions they are taking.

In the interest of full disclosure, it is important for me to point out that there is more than one type of matrix that can be used at the top of this chart. The matrix type used depends on the method you choose to reach this point in the planning process. Some will choose to reach this point through the development of an IT Vision. (See my book "How to Create A Great Information Technology Vision – And Thrill your CEO) and use the matrix in that book. The important thing is to create a one-page document that is the simple motivational description of the goal and how the team is going to reach that goal.

If this process is followed, there will have been an extensive amount of background research done by team members to develop the Strategic Target. However, this one-page document that results from all the planning and research is the simple tool everyone will refer to as the team moves forward. In my experience, a well-led team, clearly briefed on the Strategic Target and the meaning of this one-page chart, will aggressively and enthusiastically accomplish their mission.

People will meet your expectations.

Remember that the first and most important rule of leadership is that "People will meet your expectations". This one-page leadership document sets the expectation of success. It keeps the Strategic Target in full, clear view in simple terms.

It is clear to all of us that there is a lot of work behind this one-page document. The work involves a close partnership between the CIO's team and the core enterprise planners. The IT team must make a great effort to fully understand the Enterprise Vision and Infrastructure and ensure that an Information Technology Vision and Infrastructure is created that supports and enhances the enterprise objectives. The CIO must be a true leader who excites the team and leads them to be consciously competent so they can reach absolute success.

There was also a lot of work that resulted from President Kennedy's simply stated vision of "before this decade is out of landing a man on the moon and returning him safely to earth". He stated an expectation, and the nation met his expectation!

The one-page planning document defined here sets an expectation that is clear and concise and can be easily made visible to all. It provides an achievable Technology Vision that is fully based on, supports, and enhances the Enterprise Vision and Infrastructure established by the enterprise executive team.

Keeping it Going

Continuous Improvement Process

 Continuous Improvement Process

- Involves Business and Technology leaders inside and outside your organization
- Involves people inside and outside your organization who have and can define a clear vision of the future

Never Make a Design Decision for Only One Reason!

© IT Vision Consulting

As mentioned earlier, strategic planning is not simple. There are only a few technologists who have the combination of business acumen and technical experience to create the evolving set of Tactical steps needed to take an organization from a current operational platform to a moving Strategic Target. In all probability, this continuous improvement process for strategic planning will have to involve business and technology leaders inside and outside your organization who

84

have, and can define, a clear Vision for the future. The top leaders in your organization will have to lead the effort with enthusiasm, actively promote and sell the Vision, and visibly expect success. In the end, everyone involved will meet the expectations of these leaders.

Partnership In Planning

Partnership in Planning

- Integrated Planning is not simple or easy
- Partnerships between your organization and other companies may be beneficial or even necessary
  - Business planning
  - Technology planning

® IT Vision Consulting

At a high level, this process is easy to define and explain. However, integrated planning is challenging. It requires a broad set of business and technical skills ranging from long-term planning to daily operations. This planning must be a team effort with each of the players conscientiously and effectively playing their assigned position. Most of the people

85

in an enterprise are focused on daily or near term activities. Very few are routinely looking at the distant objectives. Given the pace of information technology this may be more true of the IT and MIS teams. Sometimes it is tough for the CIO's team to understand what is happening even six months to a year down the road.

It is necessary to make sure that the technology people inside the organization work to understand the detailed business needs of the various divisions and establish close relationships with those divisions.

In the past, I have carefully chosen outside business partners to work with internal people to develop and support the Business Vision and Integrated Infrastructure through the planning horizon. Any clear view of the more distant future at the planning horizon might only be gained through trusted partnerships with one or more vendors who are delivering the technologies needed by the enterprise. These vendors can provide intimate, and often non-disclosure, views of the work going on in their companies. These revelations will go a long way toward helping to define the elements of the Strategic Target and the evolutionary path to that target.

Leadership and Expectations

- This isn't easy stuff! But it works!
- The top leaders will have to
  - Lead this effort with enthusiasm
  - Promote the vision
  - Visibly expect success

--ITVC First Rule of Leadership--
People Will Meet Your Expectations!

® IT Vision Consulting

None of this is easy stuff. However, it works if applied on a continuous basis. The top business and technical element executives will have to lead this effort with enthusiasm. They will have to be the chief sales people of the Vision promoting it in staff meetings, in hallway discussions and trips to manufacturing, sales and operations locations. These executives will have to make it known that they expect success, and that they believe their teams have the talent to achieve that success.

People will meet your expectations, whether they are high or low!

87

Achieve Absolute Success!

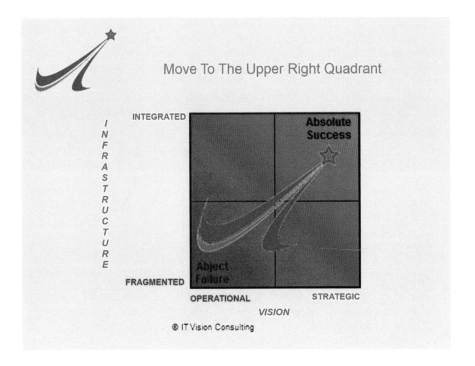

Move To The Upper Right Quadrant

In summary, those who have a clearly stated, simply explainable Strategic Vision placed at some point which is probably several years into the future will be leading a team that is reaching its objectives successfully, with minimal cost and providing great customer satisfaction.

Leaders who produce a Strategic Vision have a much greater chance of developing an Integrated Infrastructure and a successful organization in the long run. They will achieve Absolute Success!

Reach The Strategic Target and Absolute Success!

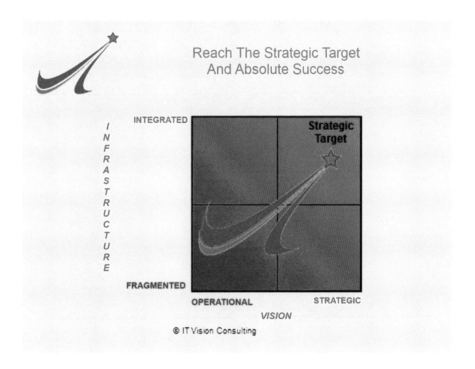

Reach The Strategic Target
And Absolute Success

® IT Vision Consulting

A Strategic Target can only be established for the organization if there is a clear Strategic Vision and a well-Integrated Infrastructure. This gives everyone in the organization something to "shoot at". Without a Strategic Target, the organization will end up somewhere in the yellow zone and perhaps be a mediocre player. With the appropriate planning intervals, new Strategic Targets can be reestablished at various times. Mid-course corrections can be made that keep the Tactical Path to the Strategic Target as linear as possible leading to an optimal cost of operation. The excellent

89

Information Technology planning team will contribute to keeping costs low, improve margins and help make the company a leader in its industry.

About The Author

Tom Ireland has a BS in Electronics Engineering and a minor in mathematics from Oklahoma State University.

Upon graduating from college, Tom accepted a commission in the United States Air Force where he served in several capacities in Turkey and North America. Along with other duties, he worked as a technology program manager while an Air Force Officer and Department of Defense Civilian.

After federal service he went to work for a technology division of the Mead Corporation responsible for designing and operating their networks in support of what was at that time the world's largest on-line, full-text search and retrieval database. Tom then moved to Mead Corporate Staff where he successfully integrated their network operations. He directed the modernization of, and assumed operational responsibility for, the corporation's client services systems. At Mead, he was asked to participate in a Vision Team which successfully established a long term IT Vision for the corporation.

Tom later went to work for CompuServe/UUNet. Over the course of three years, he fully integrated the operations of their web hosting data centers while the operation was expanding from three to twenty data centers across North America.

Tom has been featured in a cover article in "Wireless for the Corporate User" and has been published in "Telecommunications Magazine" and "Community Media Review". He is co-author of an AT&T Labs paper presented in Munich, served as the Bell Labs liaison for the Mead Corporation and has been personally highlighted in an AT&T annual report as an example of collaborative customer innovation.

2776397R00055

Made in the USA
San Bernardino, CA
03 June 2013